Fact Finders®

The Story of the
American Revolution

Great Women of the American Revolution

by Brianna Hall

Consultant:
Philip Bigler
Former Director, The James Madison Center
Harrisonburg, Virginia

CAPSTONE PRESS
a capstone imprint

Fact Finders are published by Capstone Press,
1710 Roe Crest Drive, North Mankato, Minnesota 56003.
www.capstonepub.com

Library of Congress Cataloging-in-Publication Data
Hall, Brianna.
  Great women of the American Revolution / by Brianna Hall.
    p. cm.—(Fact finders—the story of the American Revolution)
  Includes bibliographical references and index.
  Summary: "Describes notable women and women's roles in the American
    Revolution"—Provided by publisher.
  ISBN 978-1-4296-8451-4 (library binding)
  ISBN 978-1-4296-9284-7 (paperback)
  ISBN 978-1-62065-245-9 (eBook PDF)
  1. United States—History—Revolution, 1775-1783—Women—Juvenile literature.
    2. United States—History—Revolution, 1775-1783—Biography—Juvenile
    literature. 3. Women—United States—Biography—Juvenile literature. 4. Camp
    followers—United States—History—18th century—Juvenile literature. I. Title.
E276.H35 2013
973.3082—dc23

                                   2012010867

Editorial Credits
Jennifer Besel and Lori Shores, editors; Heidi Thompson and Kyle Grenz, designers;
    Wanda Winch, media researcher; Laura Manthe, production specialist

Photo Credits
Alamy: North Wind Picture Archives, 6, 18; The Bridgeman Art Library
International: © Look and Learn/Private Collection/Clive Upton, 16; Corbis:
Bettmann, cover, 4, 8, 12, 21, 29; Courtesy of Clipart ETC, Florida Center for
Instructional Technology, USF, 20; Getty Images/National Geographic/Louis S.
Glanzman, 7, 26; The Granger Collection, NYC, 24; Library of Congress: Prints
and Photographs Division, 13, 19, 22, 23; New York Public Library: Picture
Collection/Astor, Lenox and Tilden Foundations, 5; Newscom: Picture History, 9;
Pamela Patrick White, www.ppatrickwhite.com, 10, 11; Shutterstock: Christophe
Boisson, design element; www.historicalimagebank.com Painting by Don
Troiani, 14, 17

Printed in the United States of America in Brainerd, Minnesota.
032012   006672BANGF12

Table of Contents

Direct quotations appear on the following pages:

Page 9, from *The American Revolution* by David F. Burg (New York: Facts on File, 2007.)

Page 11, from *The New American Revolution Handbook* by Theodore P. Savas (New York: Savas Beatie, 2010.)

Page 14, from *Noble Deeds of American Women,* J. Clement, ed. (New York: Arno Press, 1974, 2012.)

Page 16, from *More than Petticoats: Remarkable Massachusetts Women* by Lura Rogers Seavey (Guilford, Conn.: TwoDot, 2004.)

CHAPTER 1

Everyday Heroines

Life was difficult in Great Britain's American colonies. Women, men, and children worked hard every day just to get by. Women worked sun up to sun down caring for gardens, animals, homes, and their families.

These women didn't look like rebels in their long dresses and frilly bonnets. Even on farms women wore fancy underskirts called petticoats. But when the British Parliament started passing unfair laws, colonial women had an important choice to make. Would they support King George III of Great Britain? Or would they join the fight for a new, independent nation?

Colonial women spun wool, sewed, cooked, cleaned, and looked after children. They also made household basics such as soap and candles.

parliament: a group of people who make laws and run the government in some countries

Who's Who in the Revolutionary War?

	Rebels	British
Major Groups	**Patriots** Colonists who disagreed with British rule and supported American independence	**Loyalists** Colonists who supported Great Britain's king
Leadership	**George Washington** Leader of the Continental army	**King George III** Ruling king of Great Britain
Armies	**Continental Army** Soldier group formed to resist British occupation; later French forces fought with the Continental army	**British Army** Considerd the most powerful army in the world at the time
Additional Forces	**Minutemen** Men who formed military forces to defend homes and towns at a minute's notice	**Mercenaries** Soldiers from other countries hired to serve with the British army

Women took risks to deliver secret messages and supplies.

Colonial women took action. Thousands took charge of farms and businesses when their husbands went to war. They supplied armies with bullets, food, clothing, and blankets. Women crossed enemy lines with secret messages. They held enemy soldiers prisoner in their homes. Thousands of women saw battle. These heroines may have appeared delicate, but they had strength inside and out. They knew that whichever side they chose, their help was needed.

heroine: a girl or woman who shows strength and courage by doing a good thing

CHAPTER 2

Writing for the Revolution

Great Britain racked up huge debts in winning the French-Indian war (1754–1763). In part the war was meant to defend the colonies. Britain's King George III decided that the colonies should help pay the costs. Colonists were forced to pay high taxes for items such as tea, cloth, and stamps.

Colonists began to grumble. They thought the taxes were unfair because the British government created them without any say from the colonies. In addition, Great Britain did not use the tax money to help the colonies. Hundreds of men and women boycotted British goods, but Britain didn't change the taxes. The colonists' grumbling grew louder and angrier.

Colonists protested new tax laws. They didn't think it was fair to be taxed without representation.

boycott: to refuse to take part in something as a way of making a protest

Mercy Warren

A witty woman from Boston did more than grumble. In 1768 British troops swarmed into Boston to keep order in the city. Mercy Warren objected. She wanted the British soldiers to leave Boston. Warren wrote about her anger and shared her opinions.

In 1772 the *Massachusetts Spy* newspaper published Warren's first play, *The Adulateur*. The play was meant to be read for its humor but not acted on stage. The play was the talk of the town. It made people laugh, but it also made them think about the issues of the day. Warren showed British officials as foolish and violent, while the Patriots were intelligent and bold. Warren kept writing throughout the war, and her plays became wildly popular. Warren's funny plays kept troops in good spirits and kept townspeople informed.

MERCY WARREN

FAST FACTS

In 1805 Warren published the first historical account of the Revolutionary War written by a woman.

Phyllis Wheatley

Another woman fueled the revolution with poetry. Phyllis Wheatley was a slave, but her owner's family taught her to read and write. They recognized she was a gifted writer from a very young age. When she was 14 years old, Wheatley became the first African-American poet and the first black woman in America to publish her writing.

Wheatley wrote poems about freedom even before the war began. She believed that all people deserved freedom. When the war began, she supported the Patriot cause. One of her poems called British tyranny an "iron chain." Another poem praised the bravery of General George Washington. For Wheatley the idea of a new America promised equality for all people, including slaves.

Phyllis Wheatley

tyranny: cruel or unreasonable use of power or control

Abigail Adams

As a child, Abigail Adams loved to read and write. This clever girl grew up to be an intelligent woman with independent ideas. Adams wanted to end slavery. She also believed that women deserved the same education as men.

As a member of the Continental Congress, John Adams helped create the Declaration of Independence. Abigail Adams wrote letters to her husband almost daily, urging him to refuse further British rule. She focused on the equality of all people, especially women. Adams believed every person had the right to speak his or her mind.

"If we mean to have Heroes, Statesmen and Philosophers, we should have learned women."
—Abigail Adams

Abigail Adams

Continental Congress: leaders from the 13 original American Colonies who served as the American government

CHAPTER 3

Women on the March

Women's words about justice, independence, and equality exploded off the page in the spring of 1775. British soldiers and Patriot rebels started fighting on April 19 at the Battles of Lexington and Concord. War had come to the colonies. Wives, merchants, and farmers all asked the same thing. "Which side are you on?"

Many women cooked meals for their husbands in camp.

Camp Followers

Thousands of women joined the ranks of soldiers, both on the British and Patriot sides. Historians call them camp followers because they marched with army camps. Camp followers were soldiers' wives, poor women, and women simply looking for adventure.They were not paid, but they received a half ration of food.

ration: a soldier's daily share of food

These tough women carried heavy loads through wind, snow, and heat. They prepared food and repaired cannons. They washed blankets and uniforms. These women were not trained as nurses, but they handled the bloody task of helping wounded soldiers.

"... it must be a consolation to our virtuous country women that they have never been accused of withholding their most zealous efforts to support the cause we are engaged in."
— George Washington

Martha Washington was the wife of General George Washington. She was not a true camp follower, but she did spend time in the camps. She spent winters with her husband in army camps, including Valley Forge. Mrs. Washington helped with cooking and entertaining officers.

The Washingtons (center, right) visited with the troops at Valley Forge on Christmas Day, 1779.

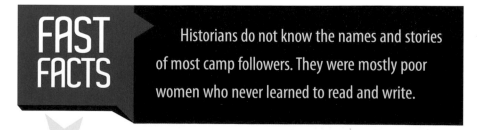

FAST FACTS

Historians do not know the names and stories of most camp followers. They were mostly poor women who never learned to read and write.

Historians believe thousands of women traveled with the army as unofficial camp followers. Many of these women were homeless and poverty-stricken during the war. These unofficial army members did not receive a ration of food or lodging. Many of these women offered cooking and sewing services for pay. Others opened small shops to sell basic items to soldiers.

Revolutionary Legends

During the war, people heard about heroism through stories. Each time a story was told, it gained new details and excitement. This is how the myth of Molly Pitcher came to be. According to most stories, Pitcher saved many Patriot lives during the Battle of Monmouth. She dodged bullets to bring buckets of water to fainting soldiers and other camp followers. In one of the stories, a cannonball passed between her legs and ripped her petticoat. In another story she grabbed a dead soldier's gun and began firing at the British.

The character of Molly Pitcher was larger than life. Although she may never have existed, the stories provide clues about what camp followers did during battle. In a way, Molly Pitcher represents all camp followers.

Margaret Corbin

Many women faced difficult decisions when their husbands joined the army. Margaret Corbin had to choose between living alone on the farm or becoming a camp follower. She decided to join her husband, John, in the army camp. During the 1776 Battle of Harlem Heights, Corbin and her husband defended Fort Washington. While he loaded a cannon, Corbin pulled wounded soldiers to safety. In a terrible instant, Corbin saw her husband shot dead.

"Margaret Corbin ... heroically filled the position of her husband, who was killed by her side ..."
—Resolution of Congress July 1779

Corbin operated the cannon until she was also wounded.

Instead of running away, Corbin took her husband's place at the cannon. She did the work of two men, loading and shooting the cannon. After the death of her husband, Corbin continued to help the Continental army and became the first woman to enlist. When the war ended, the U.S. Congress paid "Captain Molly" for her heroic work.

A Family Divided

Prudence Wright believed in the Patriot cause. But her brother worked as a British messenger. While visiting his home, Wright overheard that the British Army was coming to her hometown of Pepperell, Massachusetts. Most Patriot men had already left Pepperell to join the army, so Wright alerted the women. A force of 30 to 40 women gathered to defend the city. They dressed in their husbands' clothes and armed themselves with pitchforks and guns.

When two British horsemen approached, "Captain Prudence" commanded them to stop. She realized with horror that one of the men was her brother. She felt conflicted but did not let him go. She ordered the women to search the men. They marched the men to town and held them prisoner overnight. Wright let her brother go only when he agreed to leave the town and not return. Wright never saw her brother again.

> **"Deborah Sampson exhibited an extraordinary instance of feminine heroism by discharging the duties of a faithful, gallant soldier."**
> **—John Hancock**

Deborah Sampson

"Captain Molly" wore petticoats on the battlefield, but another brave woman dressed as a man. Deborah Sampson was 21 years old when she cut off her hair and changed her name to Robert. Joining the army was against the law for women at the time. Yet despite the risk of a fine or jail, Sampson joined the Continental army. Living as a man, Sampson trained and fought with an army of men.

Deborah Sampson served in the Light Infantry Company of the 4th Massachusetts Regiment.

During a battle near New York, Sampson was shot in the thigh. She didn't tell the doctor so he wouldn't discover her secret. Instead she tried to remove the musket ball by herself. However, she later became sick with a deadly fever. Sampson had to see the doctor. She could no longer keep her secret. Fortunately, General John Patterson recognized Sampson's loyalty and bravery. Sampson received an honorable discharge from the army in 1783.

An Iroquois Loyalist

The American Revolution also influenced the lives of American Indian women. In Iroquois culture, women are involved in important decisions, including those about war. An Iroquois diplomat named Molly Brant declared her nation to be Loyalists. She believed that defending the British would help to save her nation's land. She hoped this move would also keep their trading rights. In 1777 she rallied Iroquois warriors to help the British overthrow Fort Stanwix. Through this military action, Brant's tribe was locked into war with its Patriot neighbors.

Warriors from four of the five Iroquois nations fought on the side of the British.

diplomat: a person who manages a nation's affairs with other countries

CHAPTER 4

Spies in Petticoats

Many daring women worked undercover as spies during the war. They outsmarted their enemies to support their cause. Women were successful spies because officers didn't expect women to do such dangerous work.

Elizabeth Burgin

Elizabeth Burgin worked under the watchful eye of the British for months without being suspected. Throughout the war, British forces

held captured Patriots on awful prison ships in the New York harbor. Only women visitors were allowed. Burgin brought food to and visited with the soldiers.

Women were not suspected of gathering information for the Patriots when they spoke with British soldiers.

More Patriots died on prison ships than were killed in battles.

When a Patriot officer approached Burgin about planning a jailbreak, she agreed to help. Each time Burgin boarded the boats, she looked for escape routes and passed messages to prisoners. When the time came, Burgin informed the prisoners of the plan so they could prepare. Then, over two weeks in January 1778, she led more than 200 prisoners across the frozen New York harbor to freedom. After the mass escape, the British offered a large reward for her capture. Burgin fled New York and was never caught.

FAST FACTS

The reward for Burgin's capture was equal to 20 years of a British soldier's pay.

Emily Geiger

In the summer of 1781, Patriot General Nathanael Greene needed reinforcements. His army was retreating from a force of British soldiers. Emily Geiger volunteered to carry a message to Greene's ally, General Thomas Sumter. Greene was doubtful. Women were not trusted with such important information. But Greene was desperate, so he sent her into enemy territory. Suspicious British soldiers caught Geiger but then left to find a woman to search her. In Geiger's few minutes alone, she quickly swallowed the secret message bit by bit. The woman searched Geiger but didn't find anything, so she was released. When Geiger reached Sumter's camp, she delivered the message from memory. Sumter's troops immediately marched to help General Greene. The reinforcements led to the surrender of British troops in the Southern states.

Geiger was stopped by British scouts on the second day of her journey.

reinforcements: extra troops sent into battle

FAST FACTS

A clever Patriot spy nicknamed "Mom" Rinker hid top secret military messages inside balls of yarn. As she knitted near a cliff, she dropped them to a Patriot scout waiting below.

Ann Bates

For every Patriot spy, there was an equally clever Loyalist spy. Ann Bates snuck behind Patriot lines disguised as a camp follower. She gathered information about the Patriot army. She recorded how many soldiers belonged to each brigade, the guns used, and even the weight of their cannonballs. She sent this information to British General Henry

Ann Bates used the name "Mrs. Barnes" when she posed as a camp follower.

Clinton. In August 1778, Bates alerted the British of the Patriots' plan to march into Rhode Island. With advance information, the British forced the Patriots to retreat.

brigade: a large group of people organized for a certain purpose

Lydia Darragh

In 1777 Patriot Lydia Darragh risked her life to bring information to General Washington. When British officers demanded to use a room of her house for meeting space, Darragh was conflicted. As a Quaker, she disagreed with war and was against helping soldiers. But she knew the officers could force her out of her home if she refused. Darragh and her children would be homeless. She agreed to let the soldiers use her home.

One night the British officers met to discuss battle plans. Because they were highly secretive, Darragh suspected they were discussing something big.

Quaker: a member of the Religious Society of Friends, a group founded in the 1600s, that prefers simple religious services and opposes war

After walking several miles, Darragh ran into Patriot Thomas Craig who promised to take the message to General Washington.

In the middle of the night, Darragh snuck downstairs and crouched with her ear to a keyhole. She learned that the British were planning to attack Patriot troops in only two days.

Darragh took action. The next morning, she left for Washington's camp to inform officers of the British plans. Thanks to Darragh, the American troops were ready for the British attack.

FAST FACTS

British officers questioned Darragh after their failed attack. She told them no one was awake the night of their meeting. The officers didn't think Darragh herself could have brought information to the Patriots. They let her go without further questioning.

CHAPTER 5

Heroines at Home

As the war wore on, it spilled off the battlefield and into women's everyday lives. Patriot women helped the war effort while tending to their children, farms, stores, and homes. They sewed uniforms and prepared food for soldiers. When wounded soldiers needed aid, women cared for them. In the winter, women made blankets and warm socks for the soldiers.

Ninety-two women of the Daughters of Liberty spun 170 bundles of yarn in one day for the war effort.

Daughters of Liberty

Spinning wool was important to the Patriot cause because the rebels boycotted British cloth. For Patriot women and girls, dressing in homespun clothing was like wearing a badge of honor. Women and girls spun wool into thread for clothing. These Patriot cloth spinners called themselves the Daughters of Liberty. They gathered for spinning bees where they created thread from dawn until dusk.

Ladies Association of Philadelphia

In 1780 a group of 37 women founded a Patriot women's organization. Members included Esther Reed, the wife of the governor of Pennsylvania. Benjamin Franklin's daughter, Sarah Franklin Bache, was also a leading member. Their goal was to help make the tattered Patriot troops more comfortable.

The Ladies Association of Philadelphia began its fight by raising money. In colonial times, it was not considered appropriate for women to be involved in politics. It was even more shocking for a lady to go door-to-door asking for money. But these women raised more than $300,000, a large amount of money in the 1780s. Next they fought with needles and thread by sewing shirts, blankets, and socks for the soldiers.

Nancy Morgan Hart

The war also came to women's homes. British and Loyalist soldiers marched into homes demanding food, shelter, or money. Sometimes they burned down homes. Other times, they stole food, clothes, and money. A brave Patriot from Georgia named Nancy Morgan Hart fought back.

Nancy Morgan Hart held soldiers at gunpoint using one of their own guns.

In the summer of 1780, Loyalist troops roamed the Georgian countryside capturing Patriot officers. Six Loyalists stopped by Hart's house demanding lodging and dinner.

As the men ate and grew tired, Hart began sneaking their guns through a hole in a wall. She sent her daughter for help from Patriot troops nearby. When the Loyalists realized what Hart was doing, they tried to attack her. But Hart stood her ground and shot one of the soldiers dead. She held the remaining men prisoner until help arrived.

Eliza's Diary

Eliza Wilkinson wrote a detailed account of a British break in. In her diary, she told how four soldiers entered her home, threatening her family with swords. "They then began to plunder the house of everything they thought valuable or worth taking," she wrote. "Our trunks were split to pieces ... they took my sister's earrings from her ears; her [shoe] buckles; they demanded her ring from her finger."

A New Nation

Thanks to boycotts and battles, spying and writing, a new nation emerged. In 1783 British and American leaders signed a peace treaty. The treaty acknowledged America as an independent nation, no longer under the rule of Britain. The chaos and pain of war faded and women returned to their lives as wives, mothers, and grandmothers.

Timeline of Women's Contributions to the American Revolution

April 1775: First shots of the war are fired at Lexington and Concord.

1778: Ann Bates poses as a camp follower to spy on Patriot troops.

1776: Margaret Corbin loads and shoots a cannon during battle.

1775

1777: Lydia Darragh warns Patriots of British plans to attack.

1775–1778: Martha Washington spends winters at army camps with her husband, George.

1778: Elizabeth Burgin aids in a jailbreak to free Patriot soldiers.

History only records some of the stories of the brave women of the Revolutionary War. Countless other women supported troops and defended their homes on the frontier. They broke society's rules to become heroes. These daring women faced the dangers of war and helped to establish a new nation.

Women Intelligence Riders from South Carolina caught ememy messengers and passed their messages on to Patriot generals.

1780: Nancy Morgan Hart takes British soldiers hostage.

1782–1783: Deborah Sampson serves in the Continental army disguised as a man.

1780

1785

1781: Emily Geiger carries a secret message between two Patriot generals.

September 1783: The United States and Great Britain sign a peace treaty ending the war.

Glossary

boycott (BOY-kot)—to refuse to take part in something as a way of making a protest

brigade (bri-GAYD)—a group of people organized for a certain purpose

Continental Congress (KAHN-tuh-nen-tuhl KAHNG-gruhs)—leaders from the 13 original American Colonies who served as the American government

diplomat (DIP-luh-mat)—a person who manages a nation's affairs with other countries

heroine (HER-oh-uhn)—a girl or woman who shows strength and courage by doing a good thing

parliament (PAR-luh-muhnt)—a group of people who make laws and run the government of a country

Quaker (KWAY-kur)—a member of the Religious Society of Friends, a group founded in the 1600s that prefers simple religious services and opposes war

ration (RASH-uhn)—a soldier's daily share of food

reinforcements (ree-in-FORSS-muhnts)—extra troops sent into battle

tyranny (TIHR-uh-nee)—cruel or unreasonable use of power or control

Read More

Anderson, Laurie Halse. *Independent Dames: What You Never Knew about the Women and Girls of the American Revolution*. New York: Simon & Schuster Books for Young Readers, 2008.

Gregory, Josh. *The Revolutionary War*. Cornerstones of Freedom. New York: Children's Press, 2012.

Raum, Elizabeth. *The Dreadful, Smelly Colonies: The Disgusting Details about Life in Colonial America*. Disgusting History. Mankato, Minn: Capstone Press, 2010.

Internet Sites

FactHound offers a safe, fun way to find Internet sites related to this book. All of the sites on FactHound have been researched by our staff.

Here's all you do:

Visit *www.facthound.com*

Type in this code: 9781429684514

Check out projects, games and lots more at
www.capstonekids.com

Index